KNOWING ME, KNOWING YOU

Exploring Your Design,
Your Dating Relationship,
and Your Potential Life Together

Andrea Nelson Trice, PhD

Catalyst Publishing House
Colorado Springs, Colorado

KNOWING ME, KNOWING YOU
Published by Catalyst Publishing House
Colorado Springs, Colorado 80921

Unless otherwise indicated, scripture quotations are taken from the Holy Bible, New International Version®, NIV® Copyright © 1973, 1978, 1984, 2011 by Biblica, Inc.™ Used by permission. All rights reserved worldwide.

Cover design by Elliana G. Trice

ISBN: 978-0-578-72211-5
Printed in the United States of America

To Elliana and Nate

Answers to my prayers

Gifts from God

CONTENTS

INTRODUCTION

Life can be beautiful and filled with joy. Life can also be confusing, difficult, and heart wrenching. My goal, frankly, has always been to experience as little of the latter as possible. There are truths I wish I had known as a young adult. Some truths you must experience to learn, but wisdom can also be passed from one generation to another. In fact, the book of Proverbs is a collection of wisdom passed down from father to son.

This book began as my daughter prepared to attend college seventeen hours from home. I wanted to share life lessons with her that could provide guidance as she dated and eventually chose a husband in the years to come. The chapters draw from my background in counseling and my work as a program evaluator. They also sadly draw from my work over the past several years to make sense of what happened in my personal life as it seemingly spun out of control.

MY STORY

In April 2013, God said, "Trust Me." I did not understand the context nor the reason for this word, but I knew He had spoken to me, and I stored it away. In February 2014, my husband ended the men's Bible study he had led for several years. By May 2015, he was walking out of our home, determined to find happiness with a student less than half his age with whom he had been having an affair for the past year.

Evil dwelled in our home during that dark time and pressed against my soul. I experienced an anguish for which no words exist. Four years after my husband left, a friend and I were having lunch. She was sharing a conversation she had had with her adult daughter concerning the challenges and joys of marriage. Abruptly stopping, she began to weep as memories of all she had seen me suffer ran through her mind. I strangely became an observer in that moment. It was as if God held a mirror up for me to acknowledge, through another's tears, how profound the trauma had been.

My former husband was teaching an adult Sunday school class and serving in two ministries when I met him. People looked up to him and trusted him with leadership positions in our church. He had committed his life to Christ and was actively studying the Bible and memorizing Scripture. As we dated, he seemed like a wonderful choice for a life partner. How did he go from a seemingly loving husband and father to walking away from God and walking out on his family?

Looking back, I realize there were clues even when we were dating that cracks existed in the foundation of his faith and his life. I sought godly wisdom from several people as I prepared for marriage, but no one expressed concern. I had a master's degree in counseling and human development by then, but I was still naïve when it came to understanding how profoundly our pasts can affect our present and our future.

There are many excellent books on dating to help you prepare yourself for marriage and select a godly partner. I read those books and did the work of preparing for marriage. My life was grounded in Christ and I chose a partner whose life for many years mirrored the same priorities. So, what happened? Probably several factors were at play, but one important factor for me was naivete. I trusted too much and, coming from a solid Christian family, I had no comprehension of the extent to which childhood trauma and generational sin can affect a person if they are unwilling to pursue healing.

MY GOAL

My desire is to save you from the heartache I have experienced over the past several years as my husband ended our twenty-three years of marriage. This book is for young adults who want guidance on making wise choices as they date and eventually marry. This book is also for people like me, in midlife, who are trying to make sense of what has happened to them. It is for people who are trying to heal and make more informed choices as they begin dating again. Sometimes we can do many things right yet still end up in a place we never in a million years imagined we would be. This book is about gaining confidence to move forward from there.

As followers of Christ, we focus on life and light and hope. It can be tempting, however, to all but ignore the "spiritual forces of evil in the heavenly realms" (Ephesians 6:12). C. S. Lewis's book, *The Screwtape Letters*, was an important introduction for me, decades ago, to the Deceiver and his ways. I highly recommend that book to you.[1]

As I sat weeping in confusion and grief in 2015, my godly counselor quoted Jesus. "I am sending you out like sheep among wolves. Therefore be as shrewd as snakes and as innocent as doves" (Matthew 10:16). "Andrea," he said, "You were naïve. Do not close your heart and refuse to trust again. Do not become cynical. But do become shrewder."

[1] I have included a recommended resource list as an appendix.

3

And so began my journey to healing and to becoming more consistently aware of the prowling lion that wants to destroy our lives. Dating can be fun, but it is also a highly vulnerable time. With each chapter in this book, I hope to help you understand more about God's plan for your life as well as about the Enemy's lies that often masquerade as light. I hope to help you choose a mate who will grow closer to you as they grow closer to God through the years and who will bring you deep joy.

OVERVIEW

The focus of this book is on wise dating, but there is a foundation to your life that must be built before you build an identity with someone else. I attended a wedding soon after my husband left that vividly illustrated this for me. The bride and groom were committed Christians who met in college. The bride's vows included keeping a good home for her husband and always being there to serve him. From the beginning it seemed she would be primarily identified by her husband's work and needs. Living out her calling as a distinct child of God was apparently not part of her vision. I believe this approach limits what God has planned for each person in a marriage. It instead has one person looking to their spouse for purpose and identity rather than to God and the other person carrying a responsibility for which they were never designed.

Healthy dating relationships and ultimately healthy marriages are formed from two emotionally healthy, mature people who have spent time identifying their gifts, their unique story, and how God wants to use these in service to others. For that reason, the first half of this book focuses on you as an individual.

I begin in Part One by challenging you to take an honest look inside yourself. What do you believe about God? About yourself? Are there lies you believe that are tying you in knots? Understanding more about your deepest thoughts is an important step to becoming a healthy and mature adult.

Part Two guides you through questions that explore your unique design. What gifts or skills have others observed in you? Which of your accomplishments do you most value? What are you passionate about? Understanding and appreciating the way you were knit together empowers you to build a healthy relationship with someone else.

Part Three explores priorities to build into your life. Defining your core values and rhythms allows you to establish boundaries between who you are and who you are not. This will help you remain your own person in a dating relationship and will also make you less vulnerable to the Enemy's destructive influence.

The second half of the book then focuses on dating. Part Four offers questions designed to help you look objectively at the person you are dating and at your relationship. Past choices and current behaviors offer important windows into a person's mind and heart as do conversations around substantive topics. As the relationship becomes more serious, Part Five provides additional questions that will help you both assess your maturity levels, emotional health, and assumptions about marriage and life's purpose. Exploring these questions now will hopefully spare you unnecessary grief in the future.

This book is not designed as a daily devotional where you work through each of the topics over the course of several weeks. Take your time with these questions. Let them roll around in your mind for several days or even weeks. Ask others for their perspective. Spend time talking with God about what you are learning. Journal your thoughts. Share your insights with a friend. Let Wisdom guide you.

PART 1: WHAT'S GOING ON INSIDE?

Sometimes we jump into a story midstream, not understanding what led up to current events. Chapters in this first section begin with your beginning – exploring how your past shapes your present and your future. Questions help you explore what you have come to believe about God and about yourself. They also help you identify lies you may have come to accept as truth.

If you are a follower of Christ, your identity is defined by God. Your gifting comes from God. Past tragedies are redeemed by God. You make sense of this world by God's Truth. "For in him we live and move and have our being" (Acts 17:28a).

Dig deep and be honest as you answer these questions. Insights you gain can help you shatter lies the Accuser hopes will define your entire   life.

1 HOW HAS LIFE SHAPED ME?

If you take a developmental psychology class, you will learn about Erik Erikson. He and others have studied stages of development in our lives. These stages build on each other – if hard things happen during one stage, we may have a difficult time moving forward through subsequent stages of development. Emotionally unhealthy parent(s), trauma, neglect - many things can cause barriers to maturity. You are certainly not ruined forever if you identify a problem that has left you with unhealed wounds, but you do need to assess yourself honestly and begin the work of healing, often with others' help.

The first developmental stage is trust vs mistrust, which begins when you are a baby. Was the environment you were born into safe and secure? Were your needs met when you cried? Did you sense that you were loved and valued, or did you perceive that other people or things were a higher priority? Learning to trust safe people is crucial to emotional, mental, and spiritual health. Because your trust habits and beliefs form early in life, difficult experiences during this stage typically affect your ability to progress successfully through later life stages as well. Write initial thoughts about your childhood below.

Do an internet search and read about the other life stages. If you experienced barriers to growth during periods of your childhood, the theory suggests that you may deal with insecurity, feelings of shame, guilt, and inferiority, as well as with isolation. As I review this list, I see the Enemy's most common lies about our worth targeted at our places of greatest vulnerability. Understanding how your past affects your present is vital!

Development begins with trust - trusting others, as this theory suggests, but most importantly trusting God. Unhealed trust issues from your past can make growing your faith almost impossible. I have known several people who walked away from God as adults and almost all of them experienced pain during early childhood that they had never resolved.

Living from the Heart Jesus Gave You is a book of hope and wisdom if you are wrestling through how something in your past is affecting you now. Examine your life against the developmental stages. Pray that God would bring to your mind unresolved issues that need to be healed. If you identify an issue, seek wise counsel, and bring it into the light together.

Do not let pride make you unwilling to admit an area of brokenness and your need for healing. The Enemy desires a place of shame and fear, a place of secrecy, a crack in your foundation in which he can plant lies.

He has sent me to bind up the brokenhearted, to proclaim freedom for the captives and release from darkness for the prisoners, to proclaim the year of the Lord's favor and the day of vengeance of our God, to comfort all who mourn, and provide for those who grieve in Zion—to bestow on them a crown of beauty instead of ashes, the oil of joy instead of mourning, and a garment of praise instead of a spirit of despair. They will be called oaks of righteousness, a planting of the Lord for the display of his splendor. Isaiah 61:1-3

2 GOD DELIGHTS IN ME?

Chapter One helped you begin to explore how your past has shaped you, especially as it relates to trusting others. This chapter asks you to think specifically about your relationship with God and your level of trust with Him.

When you think about God, what image comes into your mind? Draw that image below or write words that describe how you picture God.

Thomas Aquinas defined love as "willing the good of another." Using that definition, do you believe God loves you?

With what parts of your life do you trust God?

What are ways that you specifically live out your trust in God?

With what parts of your life do you struggle to trust God?

Throughout much of my life, my answers to these questions were not particularly beautiful. As a child, I perceived God as a judge who was never pleased with me. When I pictured Him, He was distant, cold, unbending. I experienced an abundance of shame and guilt and missed God's grace and love. That made it difficult to trust God and experience joy from my relationship with Him.

Learning more about God, spending time with Him, and experiencing His faithfulness and tenderness as I walked through four painful years of infertility and then betrayal by my husband has changed how I relate to God. While I may always struggle to accept how long it can take to see God redeem hurts and injustice, trusting Him amidst suffering has truly brought me the peace that He promises.

And I pray that you, being rooted and established in love, may have power, together with all the Lord's holy people, to grasp how wide and long and high and deep is the love of Christ, and to know this love that surpasses knowledge—that you may be filled to the measure of all the fullness of God. Ephesians 3:17b – 19

3 HOW DO I RELATE TO GOD?

If God loves you, even delights in you, how do you build a relationship with Him that brings you both joy? There is not one clear path and I suspect the steps are different for each person, but here is what has made the biggest difference for me.

1. In-depth Bible studies. I started engaging in group studies by Beth Moore, Priscilla Shirer, and others in my 30s. They grew my faith and knowledge *about* God, but they also helped me *know* God in a deeper, more personal way.

2. Authors who bring Scripture to life. One of my all-time favorite authors is Kenneth Bailey because he explains the cultural context and literary tools used in a passage. After decades of reading Scripture, *Jesus through Middle Eastern Eyes* helped me think more deeply and vividly about Jesus as a real person operating in a distinct culture. The book also helped me more fully grasp His love and deep respect for women, minorities, and others who often lack a strong voice in society.

3. Learning more about God's character by studying His names. Tony Evans' book *The Power of God's Names* is a great resource.

4. Different versions of the Bible. Many apps give you free access to multiple translations. My favorites? Names of God Bible, Amplified, Young's Literal Translation, The Passion, and the Orthodox Jewish Bible. Some highlight God's various names, some highlight Hebrew and Greek wording

and sentence structure, and some, like the Passion, are poetic and emphasize God's beauty and love.

5. Regular time talking with God and sitting silently with Him. Investing in our relationship has often yielded a different perspective about problems and about His desire to walk with me through them. It has brought increased intimacy between us and increased my faith.

6. Walking through difficult times. I hate pain and frankly I hate that this is true, but painful times refine you and make you more like Christ if you allow them to do so. Nothing has been more significant in deepening my relationship with God than the times when I have hurt most deeply and made the choice to trust God through it. He truly is "near to the brokenhearted."

Relationships take time and attention. How will you continue building your relationship with God?

Write out an honest prayer to God about your desire – and perhaps your hesitancy – to deepen your relationship with Him.

And he passed in front of Moses, proclaiming, "The LORD, the LORD, the compassionate and gracious God, slow to anger, abounding in love and faithfulness." Exodus 34:6

4 WHO AM I?

What do you recognize about your unique design? List ten words that describe you.

What have others observed about you?

Which of their observations have been most valuable for gaining insight about yourself? Why?

What have you learned about yourself through books or inventories?

What patterns do you see woven through your responses to these questions?

If you have not taken the Enneagram, Myers-Briggs, or StrengthsFinder inventories, I recommend you do that. The StrengthsFinder has helped me understand why I am drawn to roles that require learning and strategic thinking and why I am willing to take significant risks to do consulting work. The Myers-Briggs has helped me understand my love for people and relationships and how I operate similarly and differently than others in my life. The Enneagram has helped me identify lies I believed and understand more about the fears and needs that can drive me.

I praise you because I am fearfully and wonderfully made; your works are wonderful, I know that full well. Psalm 139: 14

5 WHAT DOES GOD SAY?

You do not need me to tell you that people can be cruel. Always laughing backstage at their cruelty is the Accuser, also named the Deceiver. Living in a fallen world, each of us has been hurt many times. What do you do when trust has been broken? When a "safe" person becomes your enemy? God's Truths transcend – they do not have time limits on them nor qualifications. They are bedrock, the foundation upon which you can safely and wisely build your life.

What do you know about who God says you are? List all the Truths you know below.

Do an internet search on "who God says I am." Add a few more Truths below.

As a follower of Christ, you are God's child (I John 3:1), forgiven (Ephesians 1:7), and loved (Jeremiah 31:3). Which of these Truths are most difficult for you to believe? Why do you think that is?

Print out a list of who God says you are and keep it in a place where you can look at it regularly. Consider memorizing three of the verses that will bring you encouragement during hard times. My favorites include Galatians 5:1, reminding me of my freedom in Christ, Hebrews 10:19, announcing my ability to confidently enter into God's presence, and Ephesians 2:10, describing each of us as a masterpiece, God's handiwork.

God has designed you to be free and to know the joy that comes from believing deep in your soul that He loves you and delights in His relationship with you. He longs for you to know the *shalom* that comes from trusting in His goodness and from trusting that He really will redeem everything that happens to you if you will allow Him to do so.

Then you will know the truth, and the truth will set you free. John 8:32

6 WHAT'S GOING ON INSIDE MY HEAD?

The Accuser deals in darkness, silence, and shame. He seeks to isolate us and tear us down with lies. He wants to see us incapacitated, tied in knots, not realizing we are living in a prison cell whose door is wide open. We live in that space because we do not realize Christ has set us free.

Most of our thoughts are not new. Many churn in our minds over and over and tear us down. Take a few days to bring your most repeated thoughts into the light. Set your phone to go off several times a day and jot down what you were thinking at the time.

Examine your thoughts. What positive thoughts did you write down?

What negative thoughts did you write down?

Draw an image below that represents your thought life.

Think about the most painful parts of your life, the sources of greatest fear, shame, or sorrow in your life. What proportion of your thoughts are connected to these areas?

What lies may be rooted in your most frequent thoughts?

In Philippians 4, Paul challenges us to fill our minds with thoughts that are true, admirable, and beautiful. I have typically acted on this verse by focusing on thoughts that are external to me – true things others have done, beauty around me. I experience a significant internal shift, however, when I allow myself to also think about ways in which *I* am beautiful, how *I* handled myself admirably today, choices *I* made that are true. The temptation to lapse into self-righteousness exists, but I think the more likely outcome is quieting the Accuser's lies.

Talk with God about the thought patterns you are seeing. Share your observations with a friend. Talk with a counselor if that seems helpful. The battle for freedom is largely fought in our minds, but this is a topic we rarely discuss. I believe most of us never come close to experiencing the freedom God intended for us – no matter how long we live. *Into the Silent Land: A Guide to the Christian Practice of Contemplation* has helped me quiet destructive thoughts and focus on God's presence instead.

It is for freedom that Christ has set us free. Stand firm, then, and do not let yourselves be burdened again by a yoke of slavery. Galatians 5:1

7 WHAT'S BEEN HARDEST?

Understanding how your past has shaped you can lead to many valuable insights. For that reason, this chapter digs a little deeper into your history.

What are three of the hardest things that have happened to you?

How old were you when they each happened?

What stage, according to Erickson or *Living from the Heart Jesus Gave You*, were you in developmentally? Do you see evidence that you struggled to move through this stage? Is this struggle now reflected in how you view yourself or how you relate to others?

Dan Allender, in the beautiful book, *To Be Told*, offers the following observation. "More than anything else, tragedies shape our identity and our character. What are the pivotal tragedies that have set in motion the plot of our lives?... To turn away from, rather than embrace and learn from, tragedy is a double loss" (p. 87).

Have you allowed your tragedies to become part of your story? If you have kept your tragedies hidden, how is that affecting you?

Again, from *To Be Told*, "We will never come to embrace the heartache of our story until we see it profit another human being. The sorrow doesn't leave but it brings us hope with the pain and our gratitude begins to transform our past" (p. 180).

I have walked through several very difficult periods in my life. I am still healing from the last tragedy and I can testify that some of my most joy-filled moments in recent years have been sharing hope with others who are walking a dark path. Serving formally in roles that draw upon this part of my story has also been a crucial means of transforming my past.

Those who look to him are radiant. Their faces are never covered with shame.
Psalms 34:5

8 ARE THERE COMMON LIES?

Our tragedies are places of vulnerability where the Deceiver loves to focus his lies. Identifying patterns to these lies makes me more alert to and less naïve about his tactics. Genesis 3 tells the story of the Fall. After studying this chapter in recent years, I observed three ways the Deceiver tempts us all. Study the story and see if you come to the same or different conclusions.

➤ God is not good (fear)

He [the serpent] said to the woman, "Did God really say, 'You must not eat from any tree in the garden?'… You will not certainly die… for God knows that when you eat from it your eyes will be opened, and you will be like God, knowing good and evil."

➤ You know better than God (pride)

"When the woman saw that the fruit of the tree was good for food and pleasing to the eye…"

➤ You are not adequate as you are – you lack something such as wisdom (shame)

"…and also desirable for gaining wisdom"

If you keep the Deceiver's main forms of temptation in mind, you will win mental battles.

Do you see the same three temptations in this passage and in life? If not, what do you observe?

Is there one lie that plays the most prominent role in your thoughts?

What do you believe makes you most sensitive to this lie?

The lies I most often battle have elements of pride, shame, and fear all tangled together. "If I fail at this, I am incompetent." "If we disagree, I will lose your respect and therefore my value." I cannot say I have conquered the battle in my mind, but I have found that processing the lies aloud or in writing and sharing them with someone I trust has taken away much of their power. Most of the time the lies are not completely silenced, which forces me to pray and then move forward despite the fear that remains.

The thief comes only to steal and kill and destroy; I have come that they may have life and have it to the full. John 10:10

9 I BELIEVE THAT?

As I have worked through several Enneagram books, I have gained important insights and increased freedom by thinking about the Accuser's lies that are especially common for my type and how I have lived as if they were true. Below are a few lies for each Enneagram type. Once you have identified your type through an inventory, do an internet search to find additional lies that may resonate for you and start noticing how they affect you.

A free daily email I have subscribed to for years through the Enneagram Institute requires about three seconds to read, but some require weeks to process and apply. My favorite Enneagram books? *The Wisdom of the Enneagram* by Riso and Hudson and *The Path Between Us* by Suzanne Stabile.

Lies Each Type Tends to Believe

Type 1
- Making mistakes is not okay.
- I am bad, evil, defective.

Type 2
- I am not worthy of being loved.
- It is not right to have my own needs.

Type 3
- I am valuable only because of what I produce.
- I should not have my own feelings or identity.

Type 4
- I should not be too functional or too happy.
- My life has no personal significance.

Type 5
- I am incompetent.
- Pulling back from others will keep me safe.

Type 6
- I must be safe.
- I cannot trust myself.

Type 7
- Staying present to pain would destroy me.
- I cannot depend on anyone.

Type 8
- I must always be in control.
- Weakness and vulnerability must be avoided.

Type 9
- Conflict is bad and must be avoided.
- Others' desires are more important than my own.

Which lies resonate most with you?

What role do these lies play in your thought life?

How do these lies affect your emotions and behaviors?

He [the devil] was a murderer from the beginning, not holding to the truth, for there is no truth in him. When he lies, he speaks his native language, for he is a liar and the father of lies. John 8:44b

10 WHOSE BOUNDARIES?

Christians are taught to love others, sacrifice for others, turn the other cheek. This is the beautiful and difficult way of God's Kingdom. However, it is also a beautiful truth that God has bestowed each of us with dignity – and He calls us to love ourselves. Too often Christians bow to the lie that we are to focus only on others and not care for ourselves.

Boundaries are central to a healthy, balanced life. A boundary, according to Henry Cloud and John Townsend who have written several books on this topic, is a personal property line marking those things for which I am responsible. It delineates who I am and who I am not. Physical boundaries help me determine who may touch me, where, and under what circumstances. Mental boundaries free me to have my own ideas and opinions. Emotional boundaries help me deal with my own emotions and remove myself from the harmful, manipulative emotions of others. Spiritual boundaries help me differentiate God's will from my own and give me fresh reverence and awe for my Redeemer.

I did not formally learn about boundaries until my 40s. Unfortunately, I have seen that midlife is a common time to discover this crucial concept, but it does not have to take that many years!

Read quotes or a summary of Cloud and Townsend's *Boundaries* book. Which ideas are most useful to you?

Where do you need to establish stronger boundaries?

To what extent have you identified your own needs?

How skilled are you at addressing these needs?

Who might be a role model for living out healthy boundaries?

I love the passage below because it assumes it is God's will that we love ourselves. Caring for yourself is not a sin.

"Teacher, which is the greatest commandment in the Law?" Jesus replied: "'Love the Lord your God with all your heart and with all your soul and with all your mind.' This is the first and greatest commandment. And the second is like it: 'Love your neighbor as yourself.' All the Law and the Prophets hang on these two commandments." Matthew 22:36-40

11 WHAT NEEDS ATTENTION?

This last chapter of the first section gives you a chance to assess your life now. Personal coaches often use a Life Wheel as they work with a client. It divides your life into eight areas and asks you to self-rate each pie piece by shading an amount that represents its relative strength in your life. Some areas you have doubtless worked on because circumstances demanded it, but other areas may have received little attention and you would benefit from focusing on them now.

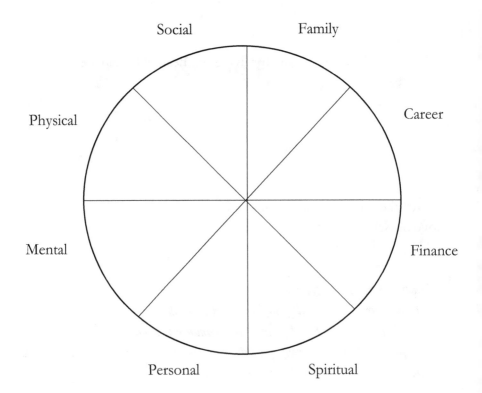

Which areas of the wheel are your strongest?

Why is that?

In what areas do you most want or need to grow?

Who or what do you need to help you grow?

For me, simply being aware of the different life areas has been helpful. I tend to be weak at addressing my own needs, so this wheel forces me to stop and think about where I am feeling pain or where I am lacking joy.

And Jesus grew in wisdom and stature, and in favor with God and man.
Luke 2:52

PART 2: HOW AM I DESIGNED?

How am I different from anyone else who has ever lived? What purpose does God have for my life?

Part Two poses questions that help you pull together what you already know about your calling, your gifting, and your interests. It also points you to inventories and other resources that can help you address knowledge gaps you may have about yourself. Enjoy learning more about how God has uniquely created you as you work through these chapters!

12 WHAT IS MY CALLING?

Vocation is from the same root word as vocal – a calling (or a summons) from God. A vocation is more than a career that uses your skills. It is more than a way to support yourself. It is investing your whole self in your work – your gifts, your experiences, your passions – and aligning your life's work with what God is doing in the world.

What do you care deeply about? The environment? Helping people connect with others? Justice? The Enneagram is a helpful resource for thinking about your passion. Interest and career inventories, such as the Strong Interest Inventory, are helpful for identifying skills as well as commonalities you share with professionals in various fields. *To Be Told,* by Dan Allender, explores calling and purposeful living from the perspective of your personal story. Gaining a clear focus to your calling may take years, but intentional reflection and prayer can go a long way in helping you identify yours.

When do you experience the most pleasure and joy?

What is it about these experiences that makes you feel alive?

What do you care deeply about?

Ask two people who know you well if they have noticed an issue about which you seem passionate.

Do your answers hint at how you could make the greatest contribution to society and uniquely glorify God?

How I live out my calling has evolved over time as I live through various experiences and gain new skills. What has remained constant is my passion to help vulnerable people regain their God-given voice. I do this through my writing, through research and consulting, and by connecting people who feel like outsiders within my local church. Who do you know who is living out their calling? Ask them about the process of identifying their calling and what they have experienced as they have lived it out.

He has shown you, O mortal, what is good. And what does the Lord require of you? To act justly and to love mercy and to walk humbly with your God. Micah 6:8

13 HOW AM I WIRED?

God calls us into work that reflects how He has designed us. As you explore calling and careers, this chapter offers you the opportunity to consider what you can learn from the roles you have already filled and the understanding you already have about yourself.

Describe three times you enjoyed what you were doing, believed you were doing it well, and felt proud of what you were doing.

What are two of your greatest strengths?

What is a significant weakness of yours?

What do you believe about your overall ability level? What evidence do you have for this belief?

How could this belief affect decisions you make about your first or next career?

How does your temperament influence the kind of work environment you will enjoy most?

I am good at pulling multiple pieces of information together and using them to paint a picture of what will likely happen in the future. I am tender hearted and experience emotional pain more easily than others. I am happy working at my desk although getting out of my office is a welcome change. As an extravert, I need to work regularly with a variety of people. These are all important insights about myself as I live out my calling on a day-to-day basis.

This chapter asks you to think not only about your past roles but also the knowledge and beliefs you have about yourself. Talk about your answers to these questions with God and with trusted people in your life. I have found that most big decisions are best made in consultation with others.

If any of you lacks wisdom, you should ask God, who gives generously to all without finding fault, and it will be given to you. But when you ask, you must believe and not doubt, because the one who doubts is like a wave of the sea, blown and tossed by the wind. That person should not expect to receive anything from the Lord. Such a person is double-minded and unstable in all they do. James 1:5-8

14 WHAT WILL I DO?

Under the umbrella of your calling are the many positions you will hold throughout your lifetime. People working today will typically engage not just in numerous positions but in five to seven *careers*. Below is a series of questions to help you identify your assumptions about this important – and ever changing - aspect of your life. It may be useful for you to talk with a career counselor about your responses to these questions.

What words or images describe the process for you of choosing a career or field of work?

Do you believe there is one right career for you at this point in your life, or do you believe several careers could tap your skills, temperament, and experiences? Why?

Does your answer increase or relieve pressure you may feel related to a career decision?

What do you most want from a career – really?

Is this a reasonable expectation?

You may notice that I titled this chapter "What Will I Do?" rather than "What Will I Be?" Americans tend to draw a significant part of our identity from our work, but this is a cultural more than a Biblical approach to thinking about a career. I encourage you to think through your answers to these questions and your career assumptions over the course of several days.

Trust in the LORD with all your heart and lean not on your own understanding; in all your ways submit to him, and he will make your paths straight. Proverbs 3:5-6

15 WHY WILL I DO THAT?

This last chapter on career decision-making explores a few more of your career-related assumptions. Bringing assumptions into the light is empowering because it allows you to understand the true basis for many of your decisions. This process can also allow you to alter your assumptions so that your decisions better reflect your authentic goals and God's priorities.

What impressions have your parents' working lives left on you?

Who will have a voice in your career decisions? Why?

What is your worst fear as you explore career options? What is a step you can take to address this concern?

If you did not care what anyone said or thought, what would you most love to do as a career?

What is most appealing about that career?

Like many consultants, I am not driven by a career ladder. Building strong relationships with important people in my life matters to me at least as much as my work. These insights help me understand past career choices, such as walking away from a tenure-track faculty position, as well as why I have chosen consulting at this life stage rather than a permanent position that would offer far more financial security.

Insights like these also give me courage to keep pursuing the work I believe God has called me to do. There is freedom and strength in understanding who God has made you to be!

Each of you should use whatever gift you have received to serve others, as faithful stewards of God's grace in its various forms. I Peter 4:10

16 WHAT ARE MY SPIRITUAL GIFTS?

Spiritual gifts are a Biblical concept. Ephesians 4, Romans 12, and 1 Corinthians 12 talk about these gifts, but in my experience a minority of Christians have identified theirs. There are several free inventories online. Take one or two and see what you think about the results. Like insights about your past accomplishments and career interests that previous chapters covered, this information is also directly related to understanding your calling.

Are the spiritual inventory results consistent with how you believe God has wired you?

If not, why not?

Have you already used these gifts to serve others? If so, did using your gift(s) bring you joy?

Did people respond positively when you used your gifts?

Was there good that came from your efforts?

Have others commented on your strengths in these areas?

These questions have been important litmus tests for me as I serve. A body of believers is incomplete when members are not using their gifts to serve each other. This is God's design. Using my gifts to serve the church has also been an important means of forming friendships and of building something more significant than I could have built alone.

Now to each one the manifestation of the Spirit is given for the common good.
I Corinthians 12:7

PART 3: WHAT WILL DESCRIBE ME?

Socrates asserted, "An unexamined life is not worth living." As you come to understand yourself, your God, and your calling more clearly, a natural next step is to determine how you will use the gifts you have received.

This section explores a variety of questions from the near- to the long-term. What is your highest priority for the coming year? What do you want your life to look like? What do you want your tombstone to say?

Wrestling with priorities and determining how you want your life to be defined is valuable work to do before you begin dating seriously. While establishing goals and disciplines is not a one-time event, having a focus for your life will help you establish healthy relationship boundaries and will help you more easily identify the kind of person you want to date.

17 WHOM WILL I CALL FRIENDS?

God is a God of relationship. He was never one God, alone, apart, aloof. He was trinitarian from the beginning, always in relationship, giving, loving. He designed us for deep relationships as well.

An important area for establishing priorities relates to friendships – who your friends are and how you invest in those relationships. Who have proven to be trustworthy friends in your life?

What traits do you most value in a friend?

How developed are these traits in you?

I have gained valuable relational skills – as well as wisdom - through relationships with people who are substantially older than me. Is there a relative, someone with whom you serve at church, or a leader with whom you might pursue a deeper relationship?

I read years ago that there are two types of people in the world – "there you are" people and "here I am" people. These categories have stuck with me because they help me identify people I want to pursue more time with ("there you are" people) and explain why I may feel lonely or inadequate after being around "here I am" people.

How intentional are you about building and deepening friendships with emotionally healthy people?

Why do you think that is?

As iron sharpens iron, so one person sharpens another. Proverbs 27:17

18 WILL I EXERCISE?

There are disciplines you can establish now that will serve you well the rest of your life. Getting exercise is a great discipline because it bolsters you mentally, emotionally, and physically. If you enjoy sports and already exercise regularly, you do not need this chapter. If you prefer the couch, let me challenge you with a few different ways to view exercise.

- ➤ Exercise can build friendships. Instead of exercising alone, ask someone you would like to know better to hike, play tennis, or lift weights with you.
- ➤ Exercise can help you stay healthy. You may not be concerned about avoiding heart disease, cancer, or diabetes at this point in your life. However, those days will come. Establishing an exercise routine now will serve you well throughout your life. Exercise also boosts your immune system which often translates into getting sick less often now and in the future.
- ➤ Exercise can be a de-stressor. Physical activity stimulates brain chemicals that lift your mood and reduce your anxiety. There have been tough times in my life when lifting weights offered an important way to stay physically strong and to feel like I was doing something to care for myself amidst an onslaught of emotional pain.
- ➤ Exercise can turn into a special time with God. I have spent many hours of my life running to praise music. Heading onto peaceful trails can move my mind away from challenges I am facing and toward God's presence and love. Walking can be a special time to talk with God about challenges I am facing and to seek His wisdom.

What is your biggest barrier to regular exercise?

What are two reasonable approaches to getting around that barrier?

Have you taken on any negative labels for yourself related to exercise or sports?

Studies show it is best to get 150 minutes of moderate aerobic activity or 75 minutes of vigorous aerobic activity each week along with strength training at least twice a week. What would it look like for you to work exercise into your schedule for a month – just to try it out?

I can do all this through him who gives me strength. Philippians 4:13

19 WILL I EXPRESS THANKS?

Amid my husband's betrayal, God impressed on me to read Psalm 50. In the psalm, Asaph writes about thankfulness as a sacrifice to God, a form of obedience to God. God asks us to do things that are for our good; His plans come from a starting point of love. As a result of reading that psalm, I decided to make thanksgiving a regular practice. During many of those dark days, it was difficult to choose thankfulness, but healing and important perspectives shifted as I expressed my thanks for what *was* and dwelled less on what was not.

Ann Voskamp's *One Thousand Gifts* is a beautiful story of the power of thanks that is worth reading!

What are you thankful for?

A list of thanks deserves its own journal. Where can you consistently write down new thank offerings to God?

When will you add to your list? A regular time each day? Each week?

Sharing your gratitude with others is powerful. Some families store their lists of thanks and bring them out at Thanksgiving to remember all that God had provided over the past year. Is there a way you could regularly share your gratitude list with others?

Give thanks to the Lord, for he is good; his love endures forever.
1 Chronicles 16:34

20 WILL I MEMORIZE?

Tough times come to everyone and mine have most often hit out of nowhere. A few of those times were so difficult that I could not concentrate enough to read, let alone memorize. Alone at night, I was indescribably grateful for memorized Scripture that would calm me, strengthen me, and protect me from the Enemy's arrows. There are parts of the spiritual realm we do not fully understand, but I can attest that speaking Scripture out loud has calmed battles in my mind and brought peace and safety to a weary, hurting soul like nothing else.

Memorizing Scripture takes time. I personally prefer to memorize passages rather than single verses. I love having the context a passage provides and being able to slowly let several verses wash over me when I am awake in the night. I also love to memorize Scripture set to music because, while our brains are phenomenal at storing information, retrieving that information can be challenging. Music provides a rhythm, a rhyme, and sometimes alliteration which helps the brain unlock this stored data.

My grandmother had dementia. One of the last times I visited her she had no idea who I was, but she sang verse after verse of hymns with me without missing a word. It will never be easier for you to memorize than when you are young, and the verses will be there for the rest of your life.

Search for Scripture songs – there are many on YouTube if you want a video. Learn a new song that speaks to you during this season of your life.

What is a challenge you are facing today? Find a passage that addresses this challenge, write it below, then memorize it.

Ask a friend to hold you accountable as you memorize Scripture. It will deepen your friendship, encourage you, and maybe challenge them to memorize with you. Who could that friend be?

Do not fear, for I have redeemed you; I have summoned you by name; you are mine. When you pass through the waters, I will be with you; and when you pass through the rivers, they will not sweep over you. Isaiah 43:1b-2a

21 WILL I GIVE?

Jesus chose money as a common teaching topic. He knew the power it could have over us and how quickly we could find money defining our priorities. Research shows that people are happiest earning about $75,000 a year. But that's just happiness. Having lived with very limited financial resources during high school and then again recently, I can testify that these periods offer you the opportunity to increase your dependence on God and to learn contentment with what you have. Both are tremendous gifts!

We insure so much of our lives against harm – we invest in life, disability, unemployment, medical, dental, vision, jewelry, auto, even umbrella insurance policies. Insurance is a good thing, but it emphasizes building a safety net that can limit our dependence on God. God loves to give and building a "fortress" for ourselves can limit how we experience God's provision. Over these past few years, God has provided in amazing ways and my faith has been strengthened.

I honestly still struggle with giving – especially because I do not have a steady paycheck as a consultant. Struggling is okay – and God wants me to talk with Him about this. The impression I come away with after praying about my struggle is that I will be limiting God's blessing if I choose not to give in faith. So, I give. I give regularly to God out of thankfulness for what He has given to me. I give out of obedience. I give to grow my faith. I give to receive His blessing.

Do you have a habit of tithing from what you earn? Why or why not?

Read verses about tithing or money and write the main ideas here.

Talk with God about your fears, your hopes, and your heart related to tithing. Write thoughts from this process here.

Decide about your giving while you are young. This is the time to establish habits that will serve you well throughout your life. Talk with a trusted friend about your decision and ask them to hold you accountable for giving. What have you decided? Why?

"Bring the whole tithe into the storehouse, that there may be food in my house. Test me in this," says the Lord Almighty, "and see if I will not throw open the floodgates of heaven and pour out so much blessing that there will not be room enough to store it." Malachi 3:10

22 WILL I BE STILL?

Fasting, praying, silence. Jesus emphasized spiritual disciplines by teaching about them as well as by modeling them. If they were important to Jesus, I think it is safe to assume they should be important to me.

As I explore and determine rhythms for my life, I begin with the assumption that God longs for a relationship with me. He loves me. I also operate with the assumption that God is faithful and will respond to my investment in growing closer to Him.

In fact, some of the most memorable and joy-filled times in my life have occurred while spending several hours with God, often outdoors, praying, reading Scripture, fasting, listening for His voice. My experience has been that sometimes God speaks during those times. He may lay on my heart a passage of Scripture to read or simply bring a Truth from His word to mind. He may wait a few days to impress a thought on my heart or there may be no word. I leave a time of fasting and prayer with the sense that our communication lines have been cleaned of debris that I have allowed to get between us. I am in a better position to hear from Him if He chooses to speak, and I have waited on Him as He calls us to do.

I try to take a retreat as I begin something new, at the start of a year, when I am working through a big decision, or when I am struggling with a problem. I am encouraged by these times and often my relationship with God is deepened. I love picturing God smiling – even grinning – as I enjoy the beauty of all He has created, His amazing Word, and the desire of His child to spend time with Him.

What thoughts do you have after reading about my experiences?

Do you know someone who is regularly still before God? Ask them about their experience and any recommendations they may have for you.

Where is a place you can go to be still before God? Will you make room in your schedule to spend extended time with God sometime in the next two months?

Be still and know that I am God. I will be exalted among the nations. I will be exalted in the earth. Psalm 46:10

Therefore, brothers and sisters, since we have confidence to enter the most holy place by the blood of Jesus, by a new and living way opened for us through the curtain, that is, his body, and since we have a great priest over the house of god, let us draw near to god with a sincere heart and with the full assurance that faith brings, having our hearts sprinkled to cleanse us from a guilty conscience and having our bodies washed with pure water. Hebrews 10:19-22

23 WILL I REST?

Taking a break from my ordinary work one day each week is an act of submission to God. It is also a habit that truly breathes new life into me.

> ➤ A day of rest reminds me of God's power and that *He* holds everything together – not me. It lifts the responsibilities of work off my shoulders for a day.
> ➤ A day of rest reminds me of all God has given to me. He has provided my work, given me gifts and skills to use in my work, and given me health and strength to be able to do my work.
> ➤ A day of rest reminds me that I am more than my work. Pulling away from my work keeps me from identifying myself too closely with it and with what I produce.
> ➤ A day of rest often renews my creativity, giving me fresh ideas and new perspectives.
> ➤ A day of rest forces me to manage my time carefully so that work does not spill over into Sunday.

Two habits I learned from others have helped me on a practical level. First, I try very hard to take a Sabbath day weekly, but it does not always have to be on a Sunday. The point is to rest, re-create, and remind myself of my submission to God's authority and care. I allow flexibility regarding the day this occurs when my circumstances require it.

Second, the Sabbath was traditionally observed from sundown Friday to sundown Saturday. Sometimes Monday morning responsibilities require that I prepare a bit on Sunday. By waiting until sundown, I can put work out of my mind all day, but also know that I have set aside time to address specific responsibilities before the day is over.

As you think about resting from work, think about technology's role in your Sabbath. I have found that resting from screens is an important part of my day. I close my laptop, leave it in my office and generally leave my smartphone in there as well. After church, I love to be outside hiking. I often play the piano and spend time with a friend or with family as well. Spending time in creation, creating something such as music, and spending time with special people in my life are intentional activities that restore my soul and move my mind away from work.

If you do not already take a weekly day of rest, what changes would you have to make to do so?

How do/would you most benefit from a weekly day of rest?

What role will technology play in your day of rest?

Keep my Sabbaths holy, that they may be a sign between us. Then you will know that I am the LORD your God. Ezekiel 20:20

24 WHAT ARE THIS YEAR'S PRIORITIES?

I have found that if I plan too far ahead, my goals grow too big and I do not reach them. If I do not plan, time usually gets away from me and I may not pursue the most important things in my life.

During this phase of your life, what are your priorities? New friendships? A deeper relationship with God? To learn more about topics you enjoy? To date a great person? Write your initial thoughts here.

My life is generally fuller and more meaningful for myself and others if I have a focus to it. Talk with God about what your priorities might be. Spend time in silence over the next several days and see if God speaks to you about this. He may not speak with words, but I have often found that asking and making room for stillness will lead to impressions, ideas that are aligned with His will as He describes in the Bible.

If you worked through the chapters in order, it may be helpful to go back to the early chapters to see what you have learned since first completing them. It may also help you identify areas where you want to focus more time. After spending a few days thinking, praying, and listening, write down additional thoughts about your priorities for this next year.

But seek first his kingdom and his righteousness and all these things will be given to you as well. Matthew 6:33

25 WHAT WILL MY TOMBSTONE SAY?

I try to live my life with the end in mind. I think this leads to wiser choices overall. As a group of people neared the end of their lives and looked back, their most common regrets included:

- Not having the courage to live my calling rather than what others expected of me
- Working too much
- Not having the courage to express my feelings
- Not staying connected with friends
- Not allowing myself to be happier

This list is drawn from *The Top Five Regrets of the Dying* by Bronnie Ware who cared for dying patients for many years.

This may seem like an impossible task, but picture yourself at 90 years of age looking back on your life. Based on what you know about yourself, how might you be answering the following questions decades from now?

What were your life priorities?

What accomplishments make you proudest?

Where did you invest too much time?

What dreams did you pursue?

When did you choose not to risk? Do you regret that now?

What brought you the greatest joy in life?

What would you like your tombstone to say?

Being confident of this that he who began a good work in you will carry it on to completion until the day of Christ Jesus. Philippians 1:6

PART 4: ARE WE WISE TO DATE EACH OTHER?

Much of this fourth section taps my evaluative skill set, as well as my counseling background, and applies it to dating. It also taps the wisdom I have sadly gained from having married a person who would, at midlife, walk away from God and from me.

In my work as an evaluator, I continually pursue answers to key questions for clients:

- What is working well?
- What would you be wise to alter?
- What is not worth continuing?

In the chapters that follow, I have written similar questions to help you evaluate aspects of your dating relationship. I also encourage you to tap common tools used in my profession as you work to better understand your relationship:

- Literature reviews – Use the body of knowledge that has been developed around a topic. If you notice potentially unhealthy behaviors in your relationship, do an internet search and see what you can learn about these behaviors. Your goal is not to replace professional counsel but to do some initial investigative work.

- Mixing methods – Use a combination of quantitative research (e.g., personality inventories) and qualitative research (e.g., in-depth conversations, observation) to gather useful information about your relationship.

- Triangulation – Combine multiple sources of evidence to confirm or reject a specific hypothesis. Seek input from friends who know you both well. Ask wise people in your life for their perspective. Look for patterns in your answers to the questions I have posed.

Chapter topics include how well you are communicating, what current friendships can tell you about each other, and boundaries. This section also revisits a topic from earlier chapters related to your past, looking for evidence of unhealed wounds.

Please do not wait until your heart is deeply connected to someone before you seriously consider whether you would want to spend your life with them. Evaluate wisely at the beginning of the relationship. Recognize the limits of premarital counseling as well. Some programs are thoughtful and wise, but others focus only on the future, emphasizing your expectations and preferences. These programs may offer tips related to communication styles, financial management, and spousal roles but they do not explore how your past influences your present nor how current behaviors may predict future choices.

Communication skills are helpful, but these skills will not produce authentic conversation if one or both people struggle with trust issues. Financial tools are useful, but they will not change a spouse who is convinced money is the path to joy or that succeeding in one's career is life's highest priority. Discussing spousal roles can produce important insight about your assumptions, but it will not change a person's heart if they enter marriage to be served rather than to serve. These are the deeper issues that will wreak havoc in a relationship and that I hope to help you identify long before you consider taking wedding vows.

Let me add one final comment at the start. The next two sections assume you have addressed unresolved issues in your own life, and that you are emotionally healthy. If this is not the case, you would be wise to work on your own issues before dating seriously.

26 HOW DO WE DESCRIBE OUR RELATIONSHIP?

Work through these questions individually then together.

What do you most appreciate about the person you are dating?

What does this tell you about your values? About his/hers?

In what ways do you bring out the best in each other?

How is this person like other people you have dated?

Would you say you are attracted to a certain type of person? If so, why do you think that is?

How do those who know you both describe your relationship?

Do family or friends have any concerns about your relationship?

What do you know about this person's past? Is someone you trust able to vouch for their integrity?

We can choose to date someone for a variety of poor reasons – to boost our self-esteem, to add to our status, to feel secure, or to fight loneliness. We can also choose to date someone to rebel against what others want or expect. Look through your answers to these questions carefully. The stakes are high. What is your primary motivation in dating him or her – really?

27 HOW DO WE HELP EACH OTHER GROW?

Work through these questions individually then together.

In what areas do you hope she/he will help you grow?

In what areas would you like to help him/her grow?

Is he/she open to growing in these areas? Why or why not?

Could you accept them if they never grow in these areas?

How are you investing in this person now?

How is this person investing in you?

Maturity moves from being unable to care for yourself as an infant to being able to care for yourself, to being able to care for yourself and another, to finally being able to sacrificially give as a parent or other caregiver (See *Living from the Heart Jesus Gave You* by James G. Friesen et al. for more on these levels.) Trauma from the past can make you believe you must care for and protect yourself because no one else can be trusted to do so. This belief leaves a person with very little capacity to care for others in their life.

Do you see evidence of immaturity in your answers to these questions? Pursue healing if this status describes one of you. If the stuck person refuses to do this work, you are unwise to remain in the relationship.

28 HOW DO WE COMMUNICATE?

Work through these questions individually then together.

Think of an issue on which you want or need to agree and describe it below. Has one of you initiated a conversation about the issue? If so, who?

How did the other person respond? Did they engage in or avoid the conversation?

If they avoided the conversation, why is that? Do not take an easy out here. Work toward full understanding of your answer, especially if you notice consistent avoidance patterns in your relationship. Hurt or mistrust are often behind these behaviors.

What happens when you cannot come to an agreement about an issue? Is there a typical path that you usually take (e.g., one person's preference/perspective is usually followed)?

Do you argue at times? If so, is one person usually the peacemaker, perhaps even taking the blame to keep peace?

Does either of you respond to conflict by using silence?

Look for unhealthy communication patterns and work to get to the root of them. They will not simply go away over time. If you notice that one person is unwilling to engage fully in conversations that involve disagreement or that one person usually bows to the will of the other, this could indicate problems with boundaries, trust, or maturity. These potential issues warrant further exploration.

29 HOW DO WE MAKE DECISIONS?

Work through these questions individually then together.

What significant decision have you made? What process did you go through to make this decision?

How does this approach to decision making reflect your temperament? Were there ways in which this approach went against your natural tendencies?

How are your values reflected in this decision? How might others' values be reflected in your decision?

What would you do differently if you had a second chance to go through the process of making this decision?

Would you call yourself a risk taker when it comes to decision making? Why or why not?

How are each of your approaches to decision making similar and different?

Why do you think that is?

Making big decisions requires time because of the many steps involved. Prayer is essential to the process of making important decisions because it is an act of submitting your will to God's, of inviting Him into your decision-making process. Reading Scripture related to your decision is an important means of understanding what God has to say about your options.

Proverbs 15:22 speaks to the importance of seeking godly counsel. "Plans fail for lack of counsel, but with many advisers they succeed." Simply wrestling within your mind and heart about a decision is essential as well. As you talk through your decision-making patterns, warning flags include quick decisions with little thought put into them, making big decisions without counsel and prayer, and an unwillingness to mature in the decision-making process.

30 WHAT DO OUR FRIENDSHIPS REVEAL?

Work through these questions individually then together.

Describe your closest friends.

How did you get to know them?

Are most of them Christians? Why or why not?

Do you feel safe sharing authentically with them?

How have your closest friends shaped you?

How have you shaped your closest friends?

Proverbs speaks many times about friendships. Proverbs 13:20 says, "Walk with the wise and become wise, for a companion of fools suffers harm." Proverbs 22:24-25 offers, "Do not make friends with a hot-tempered person, do not associate with one easily angered, or you may learn their ways and get yourself ensnared."

Friendships reveal important things about us. Get to know friends of the person you are dating, use your observational skills, reflect on your own friends. Use this rich source of data to learn more about each other – and about yourself.

31 WHAT ABOUT PREVIOUS RELATIONSHIPS?

Work through these questions individually then together.

How would you characterize your prior experiences with dating?

Do you generally choose emotionally healthy people to date?

How is this relationship different from previous relationships? How is it similar?

Have you had a previous serious relationship? Why did it end? How did it end? How long ago was that?

What did you learn from that relationship? How are you using this knowledge in your present relationship?

If you have broken off a relationship, do you have any regrets about how you treated the person you were dating? Have you asked for forgiveness if that would be appropriate?

Take these questions seriously and consider asking for input from people who know each of you well. The course of past relationships can reveal unhealthy assumptions one of you holds about dating, unhealed wounds you have suffered, and just plain selfishness. If the person you are dating behaved poorly in a previous relationship, be careful not to assume they have grown since that time and would never act the same way toward you. Look for solid evidence of change if their behavior lacked integrity or maturity.

32 WHAT ARE HEALTHY BOUNDARIES NOW?

Work through these questions individually then together.

How long were you dating before you began a physical relationship – even just hand holding? Do you think this approach was wise or unwise?

Have you decided on appropriate boundaries for your physical relationship now? If so, what did you base your decision upon?

If you have not decided on appropriate boundaries, why not?

Do you feel pressured to become more involved physically than you believe is right? Has the person you are dating expressed a sense of entitlement for more? Entitlement is a very dangerous attitude that often signals far bigger issues inside a person. Do not ignore this warning sign.

If you have read Bible passages, Christian books on dating, or been part of a youth group, you have hopefully heard the truth that God intended sex exclusively for marriage for numerous reasons that are for our good. I appreciate Dan Allender's perspective on this topic in *To Be Told.*

"Sex without the prior expression of loyalty and commitment loses all meaning because it lacks memory of the past or promise of a future...It may well be mutually agreed upon and highly pleasurable for both participants, but it lacks trust" (p. 84-85).

I will only touch on two practical benefits of physical boundaries that relate to evaluating your relationship. A physical relationship can quickly become a primary means of communicating our feelings and our level of commitment to each other. The problem is that even a kiss can mean wildly different things to people. When words take a less prominent role and the physical relationship becomes more dominant, we end up relying on our assumptions of what the other person is thinking, which is almost always dangerous.

Connecting ourselves to another person physically can also diminish our sensitivity to warning signs about the other person's maturity level or willingness to trust. Feeling deeply connected to a person often causes us to lose our objectivity. I have known many people who found themselves married to someone who is far less than God desires. They acknowledge that the warning signs were, in fact, there from the start and might have been noted had they had the wisdom – and physical space - to look for them.

33 HOW DID CHILDHOOD SHAPE US?

Work through these questions individually then together.

Draw an image or use words to describe your childhood.

On a scale of 1 – 10, how well did your parents meet your needs? Why did you choose that rating?

How do you believe your childhood affects your relationships now?

Are you willing to acknowledge brokenness from your past and how it may still affect you? This is a sign of maturity.

As the person you are dating learns about pain from your past, are they able to respond thoughtfully to your vulnerabilities or do they only seem able to care for themselves? This is another important piece of information about them.

Jesus cared deeply about children and what happens to them. I picture Jesus expressing deep sorrow as he said, "If anyone causes one of these little ones – those who believe in me - to stumble, it would be better for them to have a large millstone hung around their neck and to be drowned in the depths of the sea" (Matthew 18:6). Childhood trauma will cause all kinds of problems in adulthood if it is not addressed. Explore together how your pasts have shaped you, both positively and negatively. Seek outside help where appropriate. "Stumbling" can take many forms which is why I believe Jesus describes the consequences of causing a child to stumble in such severe terms.

34 HOW HAVE OUR PARENTS SHAPED US?

Work through these questions individually then together.

What image or words describe your parents' marriage(s)?

What do you appreciate about their marriage(s)? What do you believe could be improved?

How would you describe your potential future in-laws' marriage(s)?

What do you appreciate about their marriage(s)? What do you believe could be improved?

If you think in terms of giving and taking in a relationship, what proportion of giving and taking would you assign to each spouse in your parents' marriages? Why do you think that is?

Are you each able to look objectively at these marriages and compare them to God's design or is one of you primarily defensive about problems that may exist in your parents' marriage(s)? This may be another important warning sign.

Contrasts are powerful, in part because they can bring to light our assumptions. Spend time together discussing those marriages with which you are most familiar. What evidence do you see of sacrificial giving? Of love demonstrated by willing the good of the other (Thomas Aquinas)? Of strength and synergies that would not exist if the two people were operating as individuals?

35 HOW HAS TRAGEDY SHAPED US?

Work through these questions individually then together.

What are two of the hardest things you have experienced in your life?

What was it like for you when these things happened?

How did you cope?

What work have you done to heal from these experiences?

How have these experiences shaped you?

How have they shaped your relationship with God?

Trauma can lead to maturity beyond your years, deeper faith, and a readiness to offer grace to others. To bring about this beauty, however, trauma must be brought into the light and addressed.

Problems occur when we are too ashamed or too proud to work through the wounds caused by deep offenses. To cope, we may have taken vows that now rule us. "I will never trust anyone again." "I will always put my needs first because no one else can be trusted to take care of me." "I will never let someone see me in a moment of weakness." Vows are one of the most dangerous results of trauma, partly because a person often does not realize they are operating under the vows nor realize their power.

Is the person you are dating willing to share, at least in general terms, about the greatest tragedies they have suffered? Are they able and willing to express how these tragedies have shaped them and steps they have taken to heal? If you meet with only silence when you try to discuss this topic, this may be a warning sign that they need to do crucial work before they are free to love and trust fully.

PART 5: WHAT WILL WE DECIDE ABOUT MARRIAGE?

The previous section on dating dealt mainly with your current relationship. It also included a look at how your pasts may be affecting the present. This last section challenges you to explore your hopes for marriage and your potential future together. Take some time with these questions and the assumptions you reveal with your answers. Let new insights lead you to new questions. Think about what is absent from your answers as well.

I again suggest that you answer the questions individually before you discuss them together. You may not have thought about these questions before and it is important to formulate individual responses rather than developing responses as a couple from the start.

36 IS COMPATIBILITY CRUCIAL?

Work through these questions individually then together.

What does compatibility in marriage mean to you?

How do you define time well spent? What seems like a waste of time to you?

Take the Myers-Briggs Type Indicator (MBTI) and an Enneagram test and discuss your similarities and differences. For example, is one of you an extravert and one an introvert? If so, how does the need for time alone differ between you and what are the implications of this difference for your relationship?

Differences can be cause for playful teasing, but do you ever feel ridiculed by your potential spouse for how you are wired?

Identify each of your love languages (see the inventory and the book by Gary Chapman) and discuss how they play out in your relationship.

One of the most beautiful marriages I have ever observed is between a man and a woman who are complete opposites on the MBTI. They readily laugh about their differences but also recognize that their opposite ways of functioning have helped them together face the challenges of raising a severely disabled child.

Being compatible is not the ticket to a happy marriage. Compatibility can mean less effort is required to maintain harmony between you, but it will not automatically create a life-giving relationship. I believe the most important result of understanding your differences is becoming aware of the work that will be involved if you choose to spend your life with someone who operates very differently from you.

37 WHAT ARE OUR PRIORITIES?

Work through these questions individually then together.

Where do you want to be in ten years with your career?

What will that require of you?

If moving is required to progress in your career, are you willing to do that? How often? Is there a point, if you have children, when you would not be willing to move?

Whose career would take precedence if a choice must be made?

What does success in life look like?

What do you believe will bring you the greatest joy in life?

In what ways do your stated priorities differ from how you are living now?

These questions get at central assumptions about life's meaning and purpose and about personal sacrifice. Have honest conversations that involve wrestling with your assumptions. To what extent are you trusting each other with your inner thoughts and fears? To what extent do your assumptions align with God's priorities for your lives? To what extent does alignment with God's priorities truly matter to you?

38 HOW ARE WE RELATING SPIRITUALLY?

Work through these questions individually then together.

How would you characterize the spiritual dimensions of your relationship? Do you pray together? Talk about God and your relationship with Him? Discuss spiritual topics? Read the Bible together?

If not, why do you think that is?

In what ways do you want your relationship to grow spiritually now?

What do you perceive to be barriers to achieving this growth?

What expectations do you have for attending church together if you marry?

What are your expectations about involvement in a small group together?

What expectations do you have for regular prayer together?

What are your expectations about regular Bible study or Bible reading?

Which practices are acceptable to submit to the other person's preferences?

Which practices are essential to you?

Sharing openly about your relationship with God and praying together requires significant trust. This is especially true if you are struggling with submitting to God in certain areas of your life. Give careful thought to the status of your spiritual relationship. It is a rich source of insight about each of your hearts and likely predicts how your spiritual relationship will look if you marry.

39 WHAT DO WE BELIEVE ABOUT MARRIAGE?

Work through these questions individually then together.

In your opinion, what was God's purpose for designing marriage from the beginning of time – even before the Fall?

What do you believe God's intended roles are for husband and wife?

Are you called to put your spouse's needs above your own always, most of the time, sometimes?

What are the implications of your answer in day-to-day life?

What are the dangers of your answer?

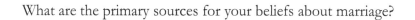

What are the primary sources for your beliefs about marriage?

How do these sources differ between you?

What are the implications of these differences?

Views vary about God's purposes for marriage. Beliefs about appropriate roles in marriage are related to beliefs about God's highest purposes for our individual lives. Spend time wrestling with answers to these questions. Pray for discernment.

I have seen people subsumed by their spouse, losing God's unique calling for their life. You are not made in your spouse's image – you are made in God's image. It is a distortion of God's purposes for your life to emphasize your relationship and service to your spouse over your relationship and service to God. This is part of the curse for women as described in Genesis 3, "Your desire will be for your husband and he will rule over you." It also reflects humanity's tendency to abuse power entrusted to us – abuse I have witnessed by both husbands and wives. Christ's sacrifice has broken the curse. Allow Him to set you both free.

40 WHAT WOULD WE HOPE FOR MARRIAGE?

Work through these questions individually then together.

Whose marriages do you most admire? Why?

What are your greatest hopes for your marriage?

What is most likely to keep you from achieving these hopes?

What are you willing to do to address these barriers?

Why would you choose this person instead of all the other people you could choose to marry?

What would marriage cost you?

Why are you willing to give that up?

I wrote about contrasts earlier. They are powerful because they can help you identify your priorities. I recall talking with a friend just before we graduated from college. She was engaged primarily because she did not want to leave college alone. I have known others who married primarily because they wanted children or financial security. From my perspective, these are reasons that can severely limit the potential of a marriage for good – if not also predict its demise from the beginning.

I see marriage as a means for God to refine each partner as iron sharpens iron, and as a means for two people to serve God in ways they could not or would not alone, including raising children together. I see it as synergy, risk-taking, and adventure, as well as beautiful companionship and support. God has amazing purposes for marriage!

41 WOULD WE INVEST IN COMMUNITY?

Work through these questions individually then together.

What are you willing to sacrifice to build a strong community with other Christians?

What do you want that community to look like?

How does the need for time with friends, both as a couple and separately, differ between you?

Are you satisfied with how you are currently negotiating this difference?

True community requires commitment, time, mutual trust, a willingness to be accountable to others, and a willingness to serve them in times of need. If one of you is hesitant to invest in a true community, explore the reasons why. Selfishness, fear, painful experiences from the past – many factors could be at play.

God designed friendships to sharpen us, strengthen us, and to bring us joy. They are a gift from God and, from my perspective, worth every minute you invest into them. Below are a few lessons I have learned, most the hard way, about building community. These apply to both individual friendships as well as to small groups.

1. Not everyone is safe. It is appropriate to vet carefully those you let into your inner circle.

2. People's level of commitment to Christ varies. It is important to have a few close friends who share your level of commitment. They are likely the ones who will sharpen you and challenge you to grow.

3. If you are going to invest in time together, invest time in going deep. Identify people with whom you feel safe and whom you respect. Then pursue intentional, extended time with them.

4. You often have more agency than you realize when it comes to relationships. If spending time with an individual or couple regularly leaves you sad or second-guessing much of what you said, these may not be safe people. We often jump to the unstated conclusion that *we* are inadequate, or something is wrong with *us* if we regularly feel hurt or shame after spending time with someone. That is a lie. If you recognize yourself in this situation, consider adding new friends to your life. Time with friends should encourage you and allow you to give and share freely.

42 WHAT WOULD WE SPEND?

Work through these questions individually then together.

How much is okay to spend on a pair of shoes? A car? A house? A vacation?

What is your attitude about debt for a car? A home? What is your basis for this attitude?

How much debt do you currently have? Do you believe this debt was wise to take on?

How do you use credit cards? How did your parents use credit cards as you were growing up? What is the relationship between your answers to these two questions?

How much of your income are you wise to save for retirement? For emergencies? For vacations?

Personal Finance was one of the best courses I ever took because understanding insurance, investing, and budgeting are important life skills. Which of you would manage your family's finances? Why?

What does it mean to live within your means?

Will you spend all the money you earn, or will you increase your giving as you increase your salary?

As you think about your money, in what ways do you behave as if you are stewarding God's resources? In what ways do you behave as if your money is yours to control?

Decisions about money reflect both your priorities and assumptions about your rights. Examine very carefully your answers to these questions. They will tell you valuable things about yourself and your potential mate.

43 WHAT ARE OUR EXTENDED INFLUENCES?

Work through these questions individually then together.

What do you appreciate about your family of origin?

What do you wish could be different?

What do you appreciate about your potential spouse's family?

What do you wish could be different?

Which of your family's values do you want to bring into your marriage?

Which values would you prefer to leave behind?

To what extent did you and your potential spouse give similar answers to these questions?

If you have talked together about your childhoods and how your past affects your present, you have likely discussed your parents' emotional health. A parent could be 60 years old yet still have maturity issues that create problems for the entire family. Encountering a potential father-in-law who is narcissistic or a potential mother-in-law who is an alcoholic or has anger issues does not mean you should run from your dating relationship. However, you cannot ignore the problem.

As a first step, can you agree together that a problem exists? If not, this is an important warning sign that the person you are dating has not fully dealt with their past. Observe family dynamics and read trustworthy material about how the unhealthy behaviors often play out in adult children's lives. Do you see evidence of this in your potential mate's life? Consider talking with a counselor about what you are learning.

A parent's issues will spill onto you, your spouse, and your marriage. Establishing healthy boundaries from the beginning and understanding how the behavior patterns often play out in relationships over time is essential.

44 WHAT ARE OUR EXTENDED DIFFERENCES?

Work through these questions individually then together.

What expectations do you have regarding holidays and other time you would spend with extended family?

What expectations does your family have for you at holidays?

What expectations does your family have for the overall amount of time you would spend with them each week, month, or year? (As you move closer to marriage, this would be a good thing to discuss with them.)

Do substantial differences exist between your two families? (This could be ethnic differences, socioeconomic differences, or it could be that one of you comes from a Christian family and the other does not.) How do you notice these differences playing out in your relationship?

If you do not share the same background, consider talking with a couple who has dealt with similar differences in their marriage. How have the differences shaped their marriage?

If you date enough people, you will likely encounter parents who do not seem excited to have you in their child's life. This could be a warning sign that God is communicating through them. Especially if they are wise people, ask for their perspective about your relationship and listen carefully to their response. Do they sense important differences between you that you would be wise to explore?

Other times, the lack of excitement you perceive may primarily relate to a parent's fears about releasing their child into adulthood and marriage. It could also be the lie that no one is good enough for their child. I recommend discussing this issue at least between the two of you and perhaps seeking outside counsel. Parents' negativity about your relationship can lead to unhealthy dynamics that last for decades.

45 WHAT ARE OUR PARENTING PRIORITIES?

Work through these questions individually then together.

Do you want to have children? If so, how many? Why?

If you would both be breadwinners, would you each continue to work after you have children? How would your careers be affected by your children?

If you both work, who would take off from work when your child needs you?

What do you believe a mother and father uniquely bring to parenting?

What do you believe are the most important investments you can make in your children?

How will you become the parent you want to be?

It is likely that you would each bring many assumptions about parenting into your marriage. You do not have enough information to answer every parent-related question now, but discussing assumed roles, overall goals, and what you would *not* do provides insight into your priorities and values.

Parenting unquestionably requires sacrificial giving. As I mentioned in the How Do We Help Each Other Grow chapter, not everyone moves to a stage of maturity where they can care for themselves as well as sacrificially care for others. Having a child will bring a spouse's lack of maturity into sharp focus.

You can heal past wounds. You can move fully into the abundant life God wants for you. Some people, however, choose never to take that risk.

46 WHAT WOULD INTIMACY HOLD?

Work through these questions individually then together.

What do you believe is God's intended role for sex within marriage?

What are your assumptions regarding what your physical relationship would be like within your marriage?

How effective do you think you would be at communicating about your assumptions? Why?

Are extramarital affairs or sexual addiction in your family histories? Discuss your answers, including how many generations these sins may go back.

Is each of you willing to fully disclose your family histories and explore together how they could impact your marriage and your children? If not, why not?

The Bible speaks directly of generational sin. Stories in Genesis, for example, follow families as members commit the same sin generation after generation. You can become desensitized to sins if they were normalized in your family of origin. If the message you repeatedly witnessed or heard as a child was that a certain type of escape will bring you pleasure or even happiness, you may be more vulnerable to believing this lie as well. You may also be more apt to believe you are *entitled* to this type of "pleasure" when hard times come if that was your family's perspective.

Bring past sins into the open. Take them seriously. Establish accountability partners to keep you safely under God's protection, authority, and love.

47 WHO WOULD HOLD US ACCOUNTABLE?

Work through these questions individually then together.

Dr. Phil has said, "People who have nothing to hide, hide nothing." What safeguards are you willing to put in place to protect your relationship? For example, will you share your phone and computer passwords with each other even before marriage?

What habits are you willing to establish when you have a disagreement? Will you commit to discussing the topic within 24 hours? Will you commit to listening and repeating back what you believe you are hearing? What other safeguards can you put in place?

Discuss the wisdom of a commitment not to talk about your relationship with people of the opposite sex (except a counselor or pastor). Is this something to which you want to commit?

If you marry, would you want to commit to share with your spouse about attractions you may have? Why or why not?

Do you know married couples who have accountability partners, friends who agree to help them keep their marriage vows? If so, discuss with them how these relationships work.

Would you consider having accountability partners? If not, why not?

Accountability within your marriage and with trusted people outside your marriage is wise to establish from the beginning. The Enemy of your souls will also be the Enemy of your marriage and he will do whatever he can to tear it apart. Build protection and safety nets into your marriage even though it may seem completely unnecessary. Satan loves it when we ignore his role in this world or when we let pride define our decisions about accountability systems.

FINAL THOUGHTS

No one enters marriage perfectly whole and mature. Instead, marriage is part of God's plan for helping us become more like Christ. But the question remains: When is it wise to end a relationship rather than continue moving toward marriage? How many warning signs are too many?

There is obviously no simple formula, but I believe at least four attributes are essential in a mate.

1. Trust. Does the person you are dating trust safe people? Have they shared honestly as you worked through this book together? Is there evidence they have healed from past tragedies that may have limited their willingness to trust?

2. Maturity. Do you see evidence of their ability and willingness to care for others? Have you observed occasions where they sacrificially offered themselves to someone? Do they seem free to give to others because they are secure in their own identity?

3. Growth. Are they intentional about growing spiritually, emotionally, and relationally? Are they willing to learn, to seek wise counsel, and to admit they were wrong?

4. Submission. Have they submitted their whole life to God or are there aspects of their life that are clearly outside of God's will?

These questions are related to some of the Deceiver's greatest lies that I have mentioned throughout this book. Does fear define them or are they able to trust safe people and trust God? Can they give sacrificially to others or are they convinced they must always take care of themselves first? Does shame define them, or do they see value in what they have to offer others? Do they recognize their need for growth and submission to God or does pride rule parts of their life?

Wrestle with the implications of your answers to these and other questions I have posed throughout this book. Seek counsel regarding topics that would benefit from outside perspective and wisdom. Make decisions that honor how God has uniquely designed you. This is important work you are doing!

I pray that this book will help you avoid the pain I have experienced and instead lead you into a healthy, lifelong marriage. I would be offering an incomplete story, however, to suggest that if you pursue God's wisdom and carefully make godly choices, you will experience only *shalom* throughout your marriage. We live in a broken world that will not be made fully right until Christ's return. As someone who has walked through several dark valleys, it seems appropriate to close with a few thoughts about the value of suffering.

When I was a young adult, I believed that if I obeyed God, I would have a safe life that was generally free of heartache. I did not bump up against the problem with this theology until, in our 30s, my former husband and I struggled through four dark years of infertility. We had done nothing to bring about this pain and no amount of obedient living was going to take it away. It was then that I wrestled through this lie with God.

A decade later, I experienced the pain caused by my husband's sins against me. Pain caused by something outside of anyone's control or pain caused by someone's sin against you – unfortunately, we are not guaranteed a life void of either tragedy no matter how wisely we try to live.

Shalom will be shattered in your life. It is natural and right to fight these times, but I challenge you to also see their potential value. According to C. S. Lewis in *Till We Have Faces*, "Holy places are dark places. It is life and strength, not knowledge and words, that we get in them. Holy wisdom is not clear and thin like water, but thick and dark like blood" (p. 50).

Having acknowledged the certainty of life's tragedies, I can also testify that God's promise to redeem whatever happens to us is true. A wise person, amid my recent chaos and pain, challenged me not to let impatience limit what God wanted to do in my life. I knew this had been a wise approach during my years of infertility and as I watch God *slowly* creating beauty out of ashes again, I can testify to this excellent advice. We cannot rush the work of refinement nor God's redemptive plans, but we can rest in the knowledge that they are always good because of His love for us.

My prayer for you in this beautiful, broken world is for the courage to love, to risk, to fully live the life God has purposed for you. I pray for you God's joy.

RESOURCES

Below is a list of the resources I have recommended throughout the chapters of this book.

Allender, Dan. (2006). *To Be Told. God Invites You to Coauthor Your Future.* Waterbrook.

Bailey, Kenneth. (2008). *Jesus through Middle Eastern Eyes. Cultural Studies in the Gospels.* IVP Academic.

Chapman, Gary. (2015). *The 5 Love Languages: The Secret to Love that Lasts.* Northfield Publishing.

Cloud, Henry & Townsend, John. (2017). *Boundaries Updated and Expanded Edition: When to Say Yes, How to Say No to Take Control of Your Life.* Zondervan.

Evans, Tony. (2014). *The Power of God's Names.* Harvest House Publishers.

Friesen, James G., Wilder, E. James, Bierling, Anne M., Koepcke, Rick, & Poole, Maribeth. (2013). *Living from the Heart Jesus Gave You.* Shepherd's House, Incorporated.

Laird, Martin. (2006). *Into the Silent Land: A Guide to the Christian Practice of Contemplation.* Oxford University Press.

Lewis C. S. (reprint 2015). *The Screwtape Letters.* HarperOne.

Rath, Tom. (2007). *StrengthsFinder 2.0.* Gallup Press.

Riso, Don Richard & Hudson, Russ. (1999). *The Wisdom of the Enneagram: The Complete Guide to Psychological and Spiritual Growth for the Nine Personality Types.* Bantam.

Stabile, Suzanne. (2018). *The Path Between Us: An Enneagram Journey to Healthy Relationships*. IVP Books.

Voskamp, Ann. (2011). *One Thousand Gifts. A Dare to Live Fully Right Where You Are*. HarperCollins Publishing.

CPSIA information can be obtained
at www.ICGtesting.com
Printed in the USA
BVHW041156141220
595684BV00014B/115